THE KOMOR COMPREHENSIVE OCD INVENTORY

Dr. Christian R. Komor

Contact information for questions regarding this copyright notice or for requests for permission to reproduce or distribute materials available through this protected material may be directed to Christian R. Komor, Psy.D., KEI Global, P.O. Box 6654, Grand Rapids, MI 49516 or dr.komor@gmail.com   www.ocdrecoverycenter.com

Library of Congress Cataloging in Publication Data

Komor, Christian R., 1959-
      The OCD Recovery Center Comprehensive Inventory

 By Christian R. Komor.
                    p.   cm.
          includes bibliographic references.
          1. Stress 2. Self-Help

 I. Title.

ISBN-13: 9781492909446

ISBN-10: 1492909440

Publisher: KEI GLOBAL
                      P.O. Box 6025
                      Grand Rapids, Michigan 49516
                      www.powerofbeingbook.com

DEDICATION

To my adopted home in Sedona, Arizona. An amazing place, and even more amazing people. I look forward to many more adventures together!

CONTENTS

INTRODUCTION

This assessment instrument was over 10 years in the making. During most of that time I was traveling the United States on seminar tours where I had the amazing opportunity to train thousands of colleagues in optimal diagnosis and treatment of Obsessive Compulsive Spectrum disorders. Occasionally we would have people with OCD in the seminar. Often the professionals in the audience were not aware of how unique it was to have someone *with* OCD teaching how to *treat* OCD. The attendees with OCD knew it for a certainty! Although I would often get standing ovations at the end of the day, it was the applause from OCDers like myself that meant the most. They knew that I "got" them. While I have great respect for my fellow mental health professionals who attempt to understand and assist people with OCD, the reality is you just can't fully get it unless you are one of us.

There are a number of paper and pencil instruments designed to gather data from people with OCD. The most common among them is the Yale-Brown Obsessive Compulsive Scale which underwent an extensive and much needed revision in 2006. The Komor Comprehensive OCD Inventory (KCOCDI) was developed from the point of view of the person with OCD. As such it focuses on collecting information that will lead to one very specific goal - assisting the individual OCD sufferer! My goal in its construction was to elicit the kind of information which OCDers have told me they want their treatment providers to have. Hopefully the KCOCDI accomplishes that.

The KCOCDI is designed in sections so that separate assessments can be made of the range of symptoms the individual is experiencing, the intensity of those symptoms, the conditions which might work for or against them in the healing process, and the presence of "Special Characteristics" as well as co-existing Obsessive Compulsive Spectrum problems.

Your feedback as a user is always welcome so feel free to be in touch. I hope the KCOCDI will be helpful for you and those you share it with.

Christian R. Komor, Psy.D.
Sedona, Arizona
Grand Rapids, Michigan
dr.komor@gmail.com

PART I: RAPID SCREENING FOR OBSESSIVE COMPULSIVE DISORDER

Before participating in the full Inventory taking this rapid screening test may assist you in identifying if you have some of the classic symptoms or signs of OCD. If you answer yes to one of the following items you should then go on to complete the full Inventory. Thank you.

I-01   Yes No   Do you have unwanted ideas, images, or impulses that seem silly, nasty, or horrible?

I-02   Yes No   Do you worry excessively about dirt, germs, or chem.?

I-03   Yes No   Are you often worried that something bad will happen because you forgot something important, like locking the door or turning off appliances?

I-04   Yes No   Are you afraid you will act or speak aggressively when you really don't want to?

I-05   Yes No   Do you often feel compelled to perform some action or thought over and over?

I-06   Yes No   Are there things you feel you must do or   thoughts you must think repeatedly in order to feel comfortable or ease anxiety?

I-07   Yes No   Do you feel compelled to wash yourself or things around you repeatedly of more often than others seem to?

I-08   Yes No   Do you have to check things over and over or repeat actions many times to be sure they are done properly?

I-09   Yes No   Do you avoid situations or people you worry about hurting by aggressive words or actions?

I-10   Yes No   Do you keep many useless things because you feel that you can't throw them away?

* If you answered "Yes" to <u>any</u> of the above please proceed to the next section.

PART II: *OBSESSION* IDENTIFICATION AND INTENSITY RATING

OCD can express itself in a wide range of symptoms. Many people with OCD have more than one. Sometimes the type of symptoms experienced may relate to developmental or life experiences, while many times the type of OCD a person experiences is completely random.

Most common obsessions – Family inheritance patterns:
- Symmetry – Autosomal dominant
- Aggressive – Autosomal dominant
- Hoarding – Autosomal recessive (Different F-MRI profile)
- Contamination – Autosomal recessive
- Sexual
- Religious
- Pathologic doubt
- Somatic
- Unacceptable Urges

Most common compulsions:
- Checking
- Cleaning
- Counting
- Confessing and Reassurance
- Symmetry
- Ordering
- Hoarding
- Repeating
- Mental Rituals

This inventory is designed to provide a detailed and wide-ranging assessment of all of the characteristics of your OCD and related symptoms. It is frequently most helpful to do this Inventory with another person who knows you well as they may have additional information to add. (At the end of each symptom area there are "Other" blanks where you can fill in any symptoms you are experiencing in that particular category.) Often people will make new discoveries about their obsession and compulsions while doing the Inventory. Mark each item you experience and then give it a rating based on how powerful that item is in your life (e.g. how much time it takes up, how much you are able to resist it and how much anxiety is attached). (Scores should be based only on the past 14 days in your experience.) At the end of each section there are instructions for tallying your scores. (Note that one does not need to have corresponding Obsessions and Compulsions.) Thank you.

II-O1 Ordering and Organizing Obsessions (Distinguish from Obsessive Compulsive Personality)
(Examples)
o Preoccupation with exactness, or perfect order
10—20—30—40—50—60—70—80—90--100
o Having handwriting be perfect or "just so"
10—20—30—40—50—60—70—80—90--100
o Compiling information, files, papers, or other items a "perfect" way
10—20—30—40—50—60—70—80—90--100

Others (describe and circle strength):

_____
10—20—30—40—50—60—70—80—90—100

_____
10—20—30—40—50—60—70—80—90—100

_____
10—20—30—40—50—60—70—80—90—100

II-O2 Religious Obsessions and Scrupulosity
(Examples)
o Having blasphemous thoughts or saying bad things
10—20—30—40—50—60—70—80—90--100
o Concern about religious beliefs
10—20—30—40—50—60—70—80—90--100
o Saying prayers a certain way
10—20—30—40—50—60—70—80—90—100
o Preoccupation with religious images or thoughts
10—20—30—40—50—60—70—80—90--100
o Fears when seeing devil symbols or associated words (e.g. "Red Devil" vacuum cleaner, red)
10—20—30—40—50—60—70—80—90--100

Others (describe and circle strength):

_____
10—20—30—40—50—60—70—80—90—100

_____
10—20—30—40—50—60—70—80—90—100

_____
10—20—30—40—50—60—70—80—90—100

II-O3 Hyper-Morality Obsessions (Distinguish from Obsessive Compulsive Personality)
(Examples)
o Excessive worry about sexual thoughts
10—20—30—40—50—60—70—80—90--100
o Extreme right and wrong, morality
10—20—30—40—50—60—70—80—90--100
o Must make sure never make errors or "lie"
10—20—30—40—50—60—70—80—90--100
o Having to get everything correct or be exact
10—20—30—40—50—60—70—80—90--100
o Fear of doing something irresponsible
10—20—30—40—50—60—70—80—90--100

Others (describe and circle strength):

_____

10—20—30—40—50—60—70—80—90—100

_____

10—20—30—40—50—60—70—80—90—100

_____

10—20—30—40—50—60—70—80—90—100

II-O3 Hyper-responsibility Obsessions (Distinguish from Obsessive Compulsive Personality)
(Examples)
o Excessive worry on others behalf
10—20—30—40—50—60—70—80—90--100
o Inability to separate own interests from others
10—20—30—40—50—60—70—80—90--100
o Having to get everything correct or be exact
10—20—30—40—50—60—70—80—90--100
o Fear of own thoughts or feelings harming others
10—20—30—40—50—60—70—80—90--100
o Continually checking for things that might hurt others
10—20—30—40—50—60—70—80—90--100

Others (describe and circle strength):

_____

10—20—30—40—50—60—70—80—90—100

_____

10—20—30—40—50—60—70—80—90—100

_____

10—20—30—40—50—60—70—80—90—100

9

II-O4 Somatic Obsessions or Hypochondriasis (Distinguish from Body Dysmorphic Disorder)
(Examples)
o Strong worries about illness
10—20—30—40—50—60—70—80—90--100
o Fear of contracting disease from other people, processes or objects
10—20—30—40—50—60—70—80—90--100
o Fears of developing a specific disease
10—20—30—40—50—60—70—80—90--100
o Gross over-interpretation of bodily sensations or appearance (e.g. imagining bumps or changes in skin)
10—20—30—40—50—60—70—80—90--100

Others (describe and circle strength):
_____
10—20—30—40—50—60—70—80—90—100

_____
10—20—30—40—50—60—70—80—90—100

_____
10—20—30—40—50—60—70—80—90—100

II-O5 Body Dysmorphic Obsessions (Distinguish from Hypochondriasis)
(Examples)
o Rumination over a particular part of the body
10—20—30—40—50—60—70—80—90--100
o Anxiety about negative reactions to one's appearance
10—20—30—40—50—60—70—80—90--100

Others (describe and circle strength):
_____
10—20—30—40—50—60—70—80—90—100

_____
10—20—30—40—50—60—70—80—90—100

_____
10—20—30—40—50—60—70—80—90—100

II-O6 Contamination Obsessions – External (Distinguish from Phobias)
(Examples)
o Excessive concern with environmental contaminantes (radon, asbestos, radiation, etc)
10—20—30—40—50—60—70—80—90--100
o Fear of being touched animals
10—20—30—40—50—60—70—80—90--100

o Fear of being touched by insects
10—20—30—40—50—60—70—80—90--100
o Becoming ill by contamination
10—20—30—40—50—60—70—80—90--100
o Diseases such as AIDS, hepatitis, sexually transmitted diseases
10—20—30—40—50—60—70—80—90--100
o Fear of being contaminated by dirt or germs
10—20—30—40—50—60—70—80—90--100
o Fear of household cleansing agents or chemicals
10—20—30—40—50—60—70—80—90--100

Others (describe and circle strength):

_____
10—20—30—40—50—60—70—80—90—100

_____
10—20—30—40—50—60—70—80—90—100

_____
10—20—30—40—50—60—70—80—90—100

II-O7 Contamination Obsessions – Internal (Distinguish from Phobias)
(Examples)
o Fears regarding own body waste products (urine, feces)
10—20—30—40—50—60—70—80—90--100
o Fears regarding non-waste body fluids (tears, saliva, genital secretions)
10—20—30—40—50—60—70—80—90--100

Others (describe and circle strength):

_____
10—20—30—40—50—60—70—80—90—100

_____
10—20—30—40—50—60—70—80—90—100

_____
10—20—30—40—50—60—70—80—90—100

II-O8 Hoarding, Saving, and Collecting Obsessions (Distinguish from intense hobbies)
(Examples)
o Excessive urge to know, remember, or keep track of certain things (slogans, license plate numbers, names, words, etc)
10—20—30—40—50—60—70—80—90--100
o Picking up items from the ground

10—20—30—40—50—60—70—80—90--100
o Must fill empty space
10—20—30—40—50—60—70—80—90--100
o Throwing things away, even seemingly useless items
10—20—30—40—50—60—70—80—90--100
o Collecting useless things
10—20—30—40—50—60—70—80—90--100

Others (describe and circle strength):

_____
10—20—30—40—50—60—70—80—90—100

_____
10—20—30—40—50—60—70—80—90—100

_____
10—20—30—40—50—60—70—80—90—100

II-O9 Harming Obsessions - Others
(Examples)
o Causing harm to others
10—20—30—40—50—60—70—80—90--100
o Making others ill by contaminating them
10—20—30—40—50—60—70—80—90--100
o Possibility of acting on unwanted impulses (stab someone, hit someone, push them into the street, drown them, etc.)
10—20—30—40—50—60—70—80—90--100
o Imagined responsibility for a car accident ("Hit and run OCD")
10—20—30—40—50—60—70—80—90--100
o Fear of blurting out insults or obscenities
10—20—30—40—50—60—70—80—90--100
o Violent or horrific images in the individual's mind causing harm
10—20—30—40—50—60—70—80—90--100

Others (describe and circle strength):

_____
10—20—30—40—50—60—70—80—90—100

_____
10—20—30—40—50—60—70—80—90—100

_____
10—20—30—40—50—60—70—80—90—100

II-O10 Harming Obsessions – Self (Distinguish from suicidal or self-harming ideation)
(Examples)
o Mentally causing harm to oneself
10—20—30—40—50—60—70—80—90--100
o Physically causing harm to oneself
10—20—30—40—50—60—70—80—90--100
o Possibility of acting on unwanted impulses toward oneself
10—20—30—40—50—60—70—80—90--100
o Doing something embarrassing or looking foolish
10—20—30—40—50—60—70—80—90--100

Others (describe and circle strength):

_____
10—20—30—40—50—60—70—80—90—100

_____
10—20—30—40—50—60—70—80—90—100

_____
10—20—30—40—50—60—70—80—90—100

II-O11 Sexual Obsessions (Distinguish from Paraphillias or Sexual Addiction)
(Examples)
o Being or becoming a homosexual
10—20—30—40—50—60—70—80—90--100
o Thoughts of sexual violence
10—20—30—40—50—60—70—80—90--100
o Fears of having or having had sex with family members
10—20—30—40—50—60—70—80—90--100
o Thoughts about molesting the individual's own or other children
10—20—30—40—50—60—70—80—90--100
o Fears of "losing control" sexually
10—20—30—40—50—60—70—80—90--100

Others (describe and circle strength):

_____
10—20—30—40—50—60—70—80—90—100

_____
10—20—30—40—50—60—70—80—90—100

_____
10—20—30—40—50—60—70—80—90—100

13

II-O12 Timeline Contamination and Calendar Obsessions
(Examples)
o Magical idea that present can be contaminated by past
10—20—30—40—50—60—70—80—90--100
o Magical idea that the future can be contaminated by the present
 10—20—30—40—50—60—70—80—90--100
o Magical idea that one's consciousness can be pulled into the past
10—20—30—40—50—60—70—80—90--100
o Continual need to review dates or preoccupation with calendar
10—20—30—40—50—60—70—80—90--100

Others (describe and circle strength):

_____
10—20—30—40—50—60—70—80—90—100

_____
10—20—30—40—50—60—70—80—90—100

_____
10—20—30—40—50—60—70—80—90—100

II-O13 Perfectionistic Obsessions
(Examples)
o Fear of saying something wrong, not saying something just right, or leaving out details
10—20—30—40—50—60—70—80—90--100
o Worry about losing things
10—20—30—40—50—60—70—80—90--100
o Worry about making mistakes
10—20—30—40—50—60—70—80—90—100
o Fears of having or having had sex with family members
10—20—30—40—50—60—70—80—90--100
o Fears of not having perfect memory of events
10—20—30—40—50—60—70—80—90--100
o Fears of losing objects or information
10—20—30—40—50—60—70—80—90--100

 Others (describe and circle strength):

_____
10—20—30—40—50—60—70—80—90—100

_____
10—20—30—40—50—60—70—80—90—100

_____
10—20—30—40—50—60—70—80—90—100

II-O14 Symmetry Obsessions

(Examples)

o Having items in environment lined up or ordered perfectly
10—20—30—40—50—60—70—80—90--100
o Preoccupation with color matching
10—20—30—40—50—60—70—80—90--100
o Making certain that events are scheduled or synchronized
10—20—30—40—50—60—70—80—90--100

Others (describe and circle strength):

_____
10—20—30—40—50—60—70—80—90—100

_____
10—20—30—40—50—60—70—80—90—100

_____
10—20—30—40—50—60—70—80—90—100

II-O15 Somatosensory Obsessions (Distinguish from Hypochondriasis and Body Dysmorphic Disorder)

(Examples)

o Upset by certain sounds and noises-clocks ticking, loud noises
10—20—30—40—50—60—70—80—90--100
o Sensitive to the feel of clothing or textures on the skin
10—20—30—40—50—60—70—80—90--100
o Intrusive nonsense sounds, music, words
10—20—30—40—50—60—70—80—90--100
o Excessive focus on bodily functions, health or physical appearance
10—20—30—40—50—60—70—80—90--100
o Unusual need to pick at seams or stroke certain surfaces
10—20—30—40—50—60—70—80—90--100

Others (describe and circle strength):

_____
10—20—30—40—50—60—70—80—90—100

_____
10—20—30—40—50—60—70—80—90—100

_____
10—20—30—40—50—60—70—80—90—100

15

II-O16 Superstitious Obsessions
(Examples)
o Fear of saying certain words because of obsessional beliefs
10—20—30—40—50—60—70—80—90--100
o Fear of using certain colors for superstitious reasons
10—20—30—40—50—60—70—80—90--100
o Fears about deviating from certain patterns of counting, walking around ladders, walking between oil spots on the pavement, etc.
10—20—30—40—50—60—70—80—90--100
o Concern with lucky and unlucky numbers.
10—20—30—40—50—60—70—80—90--100

Others (describe and circle strength):

_____
10—20—30—40—50—60—70—80—90—100

_____
10—20—30—40—50—60—70—80—90—100

_____
10—20—30—40—50—60—70—80—90—100

II-O17 Relationship Obsessions (Distinguish from reassurance-seeking behavior)
(Examples)
o Inability to let go of needing to control another person's behavior
10—20—30—40—50—60—70—80—90--100
o Extreme over-protectiveness
10—20—30—40—50—60—70—80—90--100
o Stalking
10—20—30—40—50—60—70—80—90--100
o Sacrificing self-care to be around another person
10—20—30—40—50—60—70—80—90--100
o Fantasizing continually about a relationship
10—20—30—40—50—60—70—80—90--100

Others (describe and circle strength):

_____
10—20—30—40—50—60—70—80—90—100

_____
10—20—30—40—50—60—70—80—90—100

_____
10—20—30—40—50—60—70—80—90—100

II-O18 Olfactory Reference Obsessions
(Examples)
o Intrusive thoughts about body odor.
10—20—30—40—50—60—70—80—90--100
o Social avoidance
10—20—30—40—50—60—70—80—90--100
O Excessive wearing of perfumes or deodorant
10—20—30—40—50—60—70—80—90--100
o Repetitive washing
10—20—30—40—50—60—70—80—90--100
o Repetitive changing of clothes
10—20—30—40—50—60—70—80—90--100

Others (describe and circle strength):

_____
10—20—30—40—50—60—70—80—90—100

_____
10—20—30—40—50—60—70—80—90—100

_____
10—20—30—40—50—60—70—80—90—100

II-O19 Anticipatory Obsessions
(Examples)
o Bringing to mind a "positive" thought before engaging in an action where an anxious thought would normally occur.
10—20—30—40—50—60—70—80—90—100
o Bringing to mind a "positive" word or phrase before engaging in an action where an anxious thought would normally occur.
10—20—30—40—50—60—70—80—90--100
o Bringing to mind a "blocking" or "neutralizing" word or phrase before engaging in an action where an anxious thought would normally occur.
10—20—30—40—50—60—70—80—90--100

Others (describe and circle strength):

_____
10—20—30—40—50—60—70—80—90—100

_____
10—20—30—40—50—60—70—80—90—100

_____
10—20—30—40—50—60—70—80—90—100

II-O20 Ingestion Obsessions
(Examples)
o Excessive concern about risks of certain foods.
10—20—30—40—50—60—70—80—90—100
o Excessive concern of choking.
10—20—30—40—50—60—70—80—90--100
o Fears that a food will change body physiology or chemistry.
10—20—30—40—50—60—70—80—90--100

Others (describe and circle strength):

_____
10—20—30—40—50—60—70—80—90—100

_____
10—20—30—40—50—60—70—80—90—100

_____
10—20—30—40—50—60—70—80—90—100

II-O21 Superstitious or Magical Obsessions
(Examples)
o Excessive concern about black cats
10—20—30—40—50—60—70—80—90—100
o Fear of getting pregnant from bathtub or pool
10—20—30—40—50—60—70—80—90--100
o Fear of stepping on sidewalk cracks
10—20—30—40—50—60—70—80—90--100

Others (describe and circle strength):

_____
10—20—30—40—50—60—70—80—90—100

_____
10—20—30—40—50—60—70—80—90—100

_____
10—20—30—40—50—60—70—80—90—100

II-O22 Intrusive Fragmented Obsessions
(Examples)
o Intrusive awareness of shadows
10—20—30—40—50—60—70—80—90—100
o Intrusive awareness of a particular sound
10—20—30—40—50—60—70—80—90--100

o Intrusive awareness of a specific letter or number
10—20—30—40—50—60—70—80—90--100

Others (describe and circle strength):

_____
10—20—30—40—50—60—70—80—90—100

_____
10—20—30—40—50—60—70—80—90—100

_____
10—20—30—40—50—60—70—80—90—100

II-O23 Fusion Obsessions
(Examples)
o Thoughts of illness, death or calamity are associated with many different actions such as turning on faucets, turning off lights, stepping through doorways, picking up silverware, counting, etc.
10—20—30—40—50—60—70—80—90--100

Others (describe and circle strength):

_____
10—20—30—40—50—60—70—80—90--100

_____
10—20—30—40—50—60—70—80—90--100

_____
10—20—30—40—50—60—70—80—90—100

Scoring: Add up number of items marked including those created under "Others" sections for each of the above areas _____.

Now add up the scores for those items _____. Finally divide the score by the number of areas _____

(Obsession Intensity Total)

PART III: COMPULSION IDENTIFICATION AND INTENSITY RATING

Mark each item you experience and then give it a 0-100 rating based on how powerful that item is in your life (e.g. how much time it takes up, how much you are able to resist it and how much anxiety is attached). (Scores should be based only on the past 14 days in your experience.) At the end of each section please add up you scores for that section. Thank you.

III-C1 Reassurance-Seeking Compulsions (Distinguish from Scrupulosity).
(Examples)
o Continual need to share thoughts, feelings, ideas and reactions with others
10—20—30—40—50—60—70—80—90--100
o Marked difficulty in being alone for more than short periods
10—20—30—40—50—60—70—80—90--100
o Constant questioning of others about one's own behavior
10—20—30—40—50—60—70—80—90--100
o Excessive need to repetitively ask others for reassurance
10—20—30—40—50—60—70—80—90--100
o Need to confess wrong behavior, even the slightest insignificant infractions of behavior toward others
10—20—30—40—50—60—70—80—90—100
o Urgent need to confess things to others (not limited to clergy)
10—20—30—40—50—60—70—80—90--100

Others (describe and circle strength):

_____
10—20—30—40—50—60—70—80—90--100

_____
10—20—30—40—50—60—70—80—90--100

_____
10—20—30—40—50—60—70—80—90--100

III-C2 Cleaning and Washing Compulsions
(Examples)
o Excessive or lengthy hand washing
10—20—30—40—50—60—70—80—90--100
o Showering or bathing for excessive amounts of time, often in a ritualistic way of tooth brushing, grooming, shaving, etc. that is excessive or ritualistic
10—20—30—40—50—60—70—80—90--100
o Continual cleaning of things in one's environment
10—20—30—40—50—60—70—80—90--100
o Avoidance of any objects considered "contaminated" by "germs"
10—20—30—40—50—60—70—80—90--100
o Avoidance of specific places-cities, towns, buildings-considered "contaminated"
10—20—30—40—50—60—70—80—90--100

o Concern with wearing gloves or other protection to avoid "contamination"
10—20—30—40—50—60—70—80—90--100

Others (describe and circle strength):

_____
10—20—30—40—50—60—70—80—90--100

_____
10—20—30—40—50—60—70—80—90--100

_____
10—20—30—40—50—60—70—80—90--100

III-C3 Hoarding, Saving, and Collecting Compulsions
(Examples)
o Saving, collecting seemingly useless items
10—20—30—40—50—60—70—80—90--100
o Need to pick up useless items from the ground
10—20—30—40—50—60—70—80—90--100
o Difficulty throwing things away
10—20—30—40—50—60—70—80—90--100
o Collecting large numbers of things needlessly
10—20—30—40—50—60—70—80—90—100
o Receiving complaints, reminders, or having legal problems due to too many saved items
10—20—30—40—50—60—70—80—90--100
o Has great difficulty letting go of things, sharing them, leaving them out of sight
10—20—30—40—50—60—70—80—90--100

Others (describe and circle strength):

_____
10—20—30—40—50—60—70—80—90--100

_____
10—20—30—40—50—60—70—80—90--100

_____
10—20—30—40—50—60—70—80—90--100

III-C4 Risk Taking Compulsions
(Examples)
o Inability to refuse dares made to self or by others
10—20—30—40—50—60—70—80—90--100
o Gambling for excessive lengths of time or beyond financial means
10—20—30—40—50—60—70—80—90--100

o Inability to stay away from dangerous activities (fireworks, car racing, etc.)
10—20—30—40—50—60—70—80—90--100
o Repeatedly engaging in risky sex
10—20—30—40—50—60—70—80—90--100
o Taking extreme risks which may compromise health status
10—20—30—40—50—60—70—80—90--100

Others (describe and circle strength):

_____
10—20—30—40—50—60—70—80—90--100

_____
10—20—30—40—50—60—70—80—90--100

_____
10—20—30—40—50—60—70—80—90--100

III-C5 Checking Compulsions
(Examples)
o Checking that one did not make a mistake
10—20—30—40—50—60—70—80—90--100
o Checking an aspect of physical condition such as blood pressure, or heart beat
10—20—30—40—50—60—70—80—90--100
o Checking that one did not harm others without realizing it
10—20—30—40—50—60—70—80—90--100
o Checking that one did not harm the OC sufferer with realizing it
10—20—30—40—50—60—70—80—90--100
o Checking safety of physical surroundings-locks, windows, appliances, stoves
10—20—30—40—50—60—70—80—90--100
o Checking that boxes, closets or jars are closed
10—20—30—40—50—60—70—80—90--100
o Excessive worrying that one didn't understand something one read
10—20—30—40—50—60—70—80—90--100

Others (describe and circle strength):

_____
10—20—30—40—50—60—70—80—90--100

_____
10—20—30—40—50—60—70—80—90--100

_____
10—20—30—40—50—60—70—80—90--100

III-C6 Safety Compulsions
(Examples)
o Checking one did not do something that lead to future harm
10—20—30—40—50—60—70—80—90--100
o Taking excessive steps to prevent harm to self or others-for example, avoidance of certain objects or extreme precautions to prevent unlikely harm
10—20—30—40—50—60—70—80—90--100
Others (describe and circle strength):

_____
10—20—30—40—50—60—70—80—90--100

_____
10—20—30—40—50—60—70—80—90--100

_____
10—20—30—40—50—60—70—80—90—100

III-C7 Mental Ritual Compulsions (Distinguish from Schizophrenia)
(Examples)
o Mental rituals-prayers, repeating "good" thoughts to counteract "bad" thoughts performed with the intention of reducing or neutralizing anxiety.
10—20—30—40—50—60—70—80—90--100
o Silently reciting sayings, patterns, or special words and phrases
10—20—30—40—50—60—70—80—90—100
o Counting in certain ways to oneself
10—20—30—40—50—60—70—80—90--100

Others (describe and circle strength):

_____
10—20—30—40—50—60—70—80—90--100

_____
10—20—30—40—50—60—70—80—90--100

_____
10—20—30—40—50—60—70—80—90--100

III-C8 Counting Compulsions
(Examples)
10—20—30—40—50—60—70—80—90--100
o Doing certain activities a particular number of times
10—20—30—40—50—60—70—80—90--100
o Counting items-books on a shelf, ceiling tiles, cars going by

10—20—30—40—50—60—70—80—90--100
o Counting during compulsive activities, such as checking and washing
10—20—30—40—50—60—70—80—90--100
o Adding up numbers, clock times, in specific patterns
10—20—30—40—50—60—70—80—90--100

Others (describe and circle strength):

_____

10—20—30—40—50—60—70—80—90--100

_____

10—20—30—40—50—60—70—80—90--100

_____

10—20—30—40—50—60—70—80—90--100

III-C9 Food-Related Ritual Compulsions
(Examples)
o Eating ritualistically according to specific "rules"
10—20—30—40—50—60—70—80—90--100
o Arranging food or utensils in ritualistic manner
10—20—30—40—50—60—70—80—90--100
o Refusing to eat except at certain times or under certain conditions
10—20—30—40—50—60—70—80—90--100
o Eating foods in a particular order
10—20—30—40—50—60—70—80—90--100

Others (describe and circle strength):

_____

10—20—30—40—50—60—70—80—90--100

_____

10—20—30—40—50—60—70—80—90--100

_____

10—20—30—40—50—60—70—80—90—100

III-C10 Spending, Shopping or Acquiring Compulsions (Other than Hoarding)
(Examples)
o Compulsive shopping
10—20—30—40—50—60—70—80—90--100
o Hoarding purchased items

10—20—30—40—50—60—70—80—90--100
o Shopping for excessive lengths of time or in ritualistic patterns
10—20—30—40—50—60—70—80—90--100
o Buying a great number of items due to fear of running out
10—20—30—40—50—60—70—80—90--100

Others (describe and circle strength):

_____

10—20—30—40—50—60—70—80—90--100

_____

10—20—30—40—50—60—70—80—90--100

_____

10—20—30—40—50—60—70—80—90—100

III-C11 Avoidance Compulsions
(Examples)
o Avoiding places (stores, gas stations, friend's homes) where OCD episodes have occurred before.
10—20—30—40—50—60—70—80—90--100
o Avoiding thoughts which have triggered OCD in the past.
10—20—30—40—50—60—70—80—90--100
o Avoiding actions (such as turning on a faucet or opening a drawer) which are association with OCD.
10—20—30—40—50—60—70—80—90--100
o Avoiding objects in the home or elsewhere that are excepted to trigger anxiety and obsessions.
10—20—30—40—50—60—70—80—90--100

Others (describe and circle strength):

_____

10—20—30—40—50—60—70—80—90--100

_____

10—20—30—40—50—60—70—80—90--100

_____

10—20—30—40—50—60—70—80—90—100

III-C12 Symmetry and Proprioceptive Compulsions
(Examples)
o Needing to know what is on the other side of objects, walls, etc.
10—20—30—40—50—60—70—80—90--100
o Getting "just right" feelings for certain body movements or position in space
10—20—30—40—50—60—70—80—90--100

o Need to do an activity until it "feels right"
10—20—30—40—50—60—70—80—90--100
o Preferring solid colors – avoiding patterns in clothing, carpet, etc.
10—20—30—40—50—60—70—80—90--100
 o Lining up objects
10—20—30—40—50—60—70—80—90--100
o Straightening picture frames
10—20—30—40—50—60—70—80—90--100
o Making sure clothing or makeup is the same on each side of body.
10—20—30—40—50—60—70—80—90--100
o Straightening desktop items incessantly
10—20—30—40—50—60—70—80—90--100

Others (describe and circle strength):

_____
10—20—30—40—50—60—70—80—90--100

_____
10—20—30—40—50—60—70—80—90--100

_____
10—20—30—40—50—60—70—80—90—100

III-C13 Repeating Compulsions
(Examples)
o Repeating going through a doorway
10—20—30—40—50—60—70—80—90--100
o Repeating crossing borders or State lines
10—20—30—40—50—60—70—80—90--100
o Turning car on and off
10—20—30—40—50—60—70—80—90--100
o Reading and rereading things, sometimes for hours
10—20—30—40—50—60—70—80—90--100
o Excessive writing and rewriting things
10—20—30—40—50—60—70—80—90--100
o Repeating routine activities-going in and out of doorways, repeated crossing of thresholds, getting up and down from a chair, combing hair, tying shoes, dressing and undressing over and over
10—20—30—40—50—60—70—80—90--100

Others (describe and circle strength):

_____
10—20—30—40—50—60—70—80—90--100

_____
10—20—30—40—50—60—70—80—90--100

10—20—30—40—50—60—70—80—90—100

III-C14 Superstitious Compulsions (Differentiate from Phobias)
(Examples)
o Superstitious behavior that takes excessive amounts of time
10—20—30—40—50—60—70—80—90--100
o Compulsive need to touch, tap, or rub certain items or people
10—20—30—40—50—60—70—80—90—100
o Compulsion to engaging in astrology, tarot card reading, etc. to excess – unable to stop.
10—20—30—40—50—60—70—80—90--100
o Fear of inhaling (or exhaling) when passing cemeteries
10—20—30—40—50—60—70—80—90--100
o Performing rituals related to feared numbers (e.g. #13), or words (e.g. "evil")
10—20—30—40—50—60—70—80—90--100
o Compulsive avoidance of black cats, ladders, etc.
10—20—30—40—50—60—70—80—90—100
o Needing to make the "sign of the cross" before, after, or during certain situaitons
10—20—30—40—50—60—70—80—90—100

Others (describe and circle strength):

_____
10—20—30—40—50—60—70—80—90--100

_____
10—20—30—40—50—60—70—80—90--100

_____
10—20—30—40—50—60—70—80—90—100

III-C15 Tic-Like Compulsions (Differentiate from Tourette's Disorder)
(Examples)
o Need to blink a certain number of times, in patterns or in a certain order
10—20—30—40—50—60—70—80—90--100
o Compulsive need to touch, tap, or rub certain items or people
10—20—30—40—50—60—70—80—90—100
o Breathing in certain patterns
10—20—30—40—50—60—70—80—90--100
o Need to rub soft materials incessantly
10—20—30—40—50—60—70—80—90--100
o Biting tongue, chewing lip, rubbing teeth together, etc.
10—20—30—40—50—60—70—80—90--100
o Compulsive picking at seams in clothing, chairs, books, etc.
10—20—30—40—50—60—70—80—90—100

o Staring or moving eyes in certain pattern
10—20—30—40—50—60—70—80—90—100

Others (describe and circle strength):

_____
10—20—30—40—50—60—70—80—90--100

_____
10—20—30—40—50—60—70—80—90--100

_____
10—20—30—40—50—60—70—80—90—100

III-C16 Slowness Compulsion (Differentiate from Catatonia or Primary Movement Disorder)
(Examples)
o Behaving as if in slow motion
10—20—30—40—50—60—70—80—90--100
o Excessive amounts of time taken to initiate activities
10—20—30—40—50—60—70—80—90—100
o Appears "frozen" at times
10—20—30—40—50—60—70—80—90--100
o Feeling of being "slowed down in time"
10—20—30—40—50—60—70—80—90--100

Others (describe and circle strength):

_____
10—20—30—40—50—60—70—80—90--100

_____
10—20—30—40—50—60—70—80—90--100

_____
10—20—30—40—50—60—70—80—90—100

Scoring: Add up number of items marked including those created under "Others" sections for each of the above areas _____.
Now add up the scores for those items _____. Finally divide the score by the number of areas _____

                                                      (Compulsion Total)

PART IV: CORE OCD INTENSITY AND OVERVALUED IDEATION

Instructions: This section of the inventory is designed to provide us with an overview of the general intensity of your symptoms. It is frequently most helpful to do this inventory with another person who knows you well as they may have additional information to add. Circle one response for each item with "0" representing a very low level or just a little and "100" representing a high level or a great deal.

IV-01-I   Percentage of day spent on obsessions
0—10—20—30—40—50—60—70—80—90—100 %

IV-02-I   Percentage of day spent on compulsions
0—10—20—30—40—50—60—70—80—90—100 %

IV-03-I   Percentage of day spent on avoidance of obsessions or compulsions
0—10—20—30—40—50—60—70—80—90—100 %

IV-04-I   Interference in activities and goals as a result of obsessions
0—10—20—30—40—50—60—70—80—90—100

IV-05-I   Interference in activities and goals as a result of compulsions
0—10—20—30—40—50—60—70—80—90—100

IV-06-I   Interference in activities and goals due to avoidance of obsessions or compulsions
0—10—20—30—40—50—60—70—80—90—100 %

IV-07-I   Distress from obsessions
0—10—20—30—40—50—60—70—80—90—100

IV-08-I   Distress from compulsions
0—10—20—30—40—50—60—70—80—90—100

IV-09-I   Distress directly or indirectly resulting from avoidance of obsessions or compulsions
0—10—20—30—40—50—60—70—80—90—100 %

IV-10-I   Ability to resist obsessions
0—10—20—30—40—50—60—70—80—90—100

IV-11-I   Ability to exert control over compulsions
0—10—20—30—40—50—60—70—80—90—100

IV-12-I   Ability to resist avoidance of obsessions or compulsions
0—10—20—30—40—50—60—70—80—90—100 %

IV-13-I   Feelings of Depression
0—10—20—30—40—50—60—70—80—90—100

IV-14-I   Diagnosis of Bipolar Disorder
No = 0 Yes =100

IV-15-I   Feelings of social anxiety
0—10—20—30—40—50—60—70—80—90—100

IV-16-I   Diagnosis of Schizotypal Disorder
No = 0 Yes =100

IV-17-I   Diagnosis of any Personality Disorder
0—10—20—30—40—50—60—70—80—90—100

IV-18-I   Very hard to tell obsessions not real
0—10—20—30—40—50—60—70—80—90—100

IV-19-I   Presence of or family history of tics
Some10—20—30—40—50—60—70—80—90—100 A Lot

IV-20-I   Odd OCD symptoms not on most lists
Some10—20—30—40—50—60—70—80—90—100 A Lot

IV-21-I   Multiple OCD symptoms
Some10—20—30—40—50—60—70—80—90—100 A Lot

IV-22-I   Percent of life years had OCD
10—20—30—40—50—60—70—80—90—100 %

IV-23-I   Gradual onset and chronic course to OCD
10—20—30—40—50—60—70—80—90—100

IV-24-I   Early age of onset
Very Recent 10—20—30—40—50—60—70—80—90—100 Very Early

IV-25-I   Presence of multiple conditions on Obsessive-Compulsive Spectrum
No = 0 Yes = 10

IV-26-I   Little relief gained from medication
None 10—20—30—40—50—60—70—80—90—100 A Lot

IV-27-I   Little relief from prior attempts at behavior therapy
None 10—20—30—40—50—60—70—80—90—100 A Lot

IV-28-I   Impaired daily self-care routine
None 10—20—30—40—50—60—70—80—90—100 A Lot

IV-29-I   Greater than normal fatigue
None 10—20—30—40—50—60—70—80—90—100 A Lot

IV-30-I   Difficulty managing lifestyle behaviors that lead to increased anxiety
None 10—20—30—40—50—60—70—80—90—100 A Lot

IV-31-I   Hard to break free once caught in an obsessive cycle
None 10—20—30—40—50—60—70—80—90—100 A Lot

IV-32-I   Has unmanaged addictive behaviors
None 10—20—30—40—50—60—70—80—90—100 A Lot

IV-33-I   Marital and, or parenting problems related to OCD
None 10—20—30—40—50—60—70—80—90—100 A Lot

IV-34-I   Stress for lack of financial or other needed resources
None 10—20—30—40—50—60—70—80—90—100 A Lot

IV-35-I   OCD is based in thoughts which can attach themselves to just about any action
No 10—20—30—40—50—60—70—80—90—100 Very Strongly

Scoring: Add up number of items marked including those created under "Others" sections for each of the above areas _____.
Now add up the scores for those items _____. Finally divide the score by the number of areas _____

(Intensity Total)

PART V: DEPRESSION AND LIFE SATISFACTION

Somewhere between 40 and 60% of persons with OCD are also clinically depressed and this can interfere with and complicate recovery from OCD. In answering the following questions rate (1) the amount of time during the past two weeks you have experienced the symptom and (2) the overall intensity with which you have experienced the symptom.

V-1-D   I have feelings of sadness
Never   10—20—30—40—50—60—70—80—90—100 All The Time
Not At All 10—20—30—40—50—60—70—80—90—100 Very Severe

V-2-D   I have feelings of guilt
Never   10—20—30—40—50—60—70—80—90—100 All The Time
Not At All 10—20—30—40—50—60—70—80—90—100 Very Severe

V-3-D   The future seems hopeless
Never   10—20—30—40—50—60—70—80—90—100 All The Time
Not At All 10—20—30—40—50—60—70—80—90—100 Very Severe

V-4-D   I feel like a failure
Never   10—20—30—40—50—60—70—80—90—100 All The Time
Not At All 10—20—30—40—50—60—70—80—90—100 Very Severe

V-5-D   I have thoughts about taking my own life
Never   10—20—30—40—50—60—70—80—90—100 All The Time
Not At All 10—20—30—40—50—60—70—80—90—100 Very Severe

V-6-D   I feel disappointed in myself
Never   10—20—30—40—50—60—70—80—90—100 All The Time
Not At All 10—20—30—40—50—60—70—80—90—100 Very Severe

V-7-D   I cry often, sometimes for no reason at all
Never   10—20—30—40—50—60—70—80—90—100 All The Time
Not At All 10—20—30—40—50—60—70—80—90—100 Very Severe

V-8-D   I am irritated and, or frustrated with things
Never   10—20—30—40—50—60—70—80—90—100 All The Time
Not At All 10—20—30—40—50—60—70—80—90—100 Very Severe

V-9-D   I feel I am unwanted by others
Never   10—20—30—40—50—60—70—80—90—100 All The Time
Not At All 10—20—30—40—50—60—70—80—90—100 Very Severe

V-10-D   I am lonely and, or feel isolated from others
Never   10—20—30—40—50—60—70—80—90—100 All The Time
Not At All 10—20—30—40—50—60—70—80—90—100 Very Severe

V-11-D   I receive satisfaction and, or pleasure from the things I do
All The Time 10—20—30—40—50—60—70—80—90—100 Never
Very Severe   10—20—30—40—50—60—70—80—90—100 Not At All

V-12-D   I am having trouble remembering things
Never   10—20—30—40—50—60—70—80—90—100 All The Time
Not At All 10—20—30—40—50—60—70—80—90—100 Very Severe

V-13-D   I have lost interest in people and, or pets
Never   10—20—30—40—50—60—70—80—90—100 All The Time
Not At All 10—20—30—40—50—60—70—80—90—100 Very Severe

V-14-D   I have lost interest in things and, or activities
Never   10—20—30—40—50—60—70—80—90—100 All The Time
Not At All 10—20—30—40—50—60—70—80—90—100 Very Severe

V-15-D   It is difficult keeping up with things I need to do
Never   10—20—30—40—50—60—70—80—90—100 All The Time
Not At All 10—20—30—40—50—60—70—80—90—100 Very Severe

V-16-D   I am unsatisfied with my work or career
Never   10—20—30—40—50—60—70—80—90—100 All The Time
Not At All 10—20—30—40—50—60—70—80—90—100 Very Severe

V-17-D   I feel unsatisfied with my spiritual life
Never   10—20—30—40—50—60—70—80—90—100 All The Time
Not At All 10—20—30—40—50—60—70—80—90—100 Very Severe

V-18-D   I am able to sleep well
Never   10—20—30—40—50—60—70—80—90—100 All The Time
Not At All 10—20—30—40—50—60—70—80—90—100 Very Severe

V-19-D   I am unsatisfied with my sexual life
Never   10—20—30—40—50—60—70—80—90—100 All The Time
Not At All 10—20—30—40—50—60—70—80—90—100 Very Severe

V-20-D   The thoughts I have about myself seem to be negative
Never   10—20—30—40—50—60—70—80—90—100 All The Time
Not At All 10—20—30—40—50—60—70—80—90—100 Very Severe

Scoring: Add up number of items marked for each of the above areas _____. Now add up the scores for those items _____. Finally divide the score by the number of areas _____ (Intensity Total)

KOMOR COMPREHENSIVE OCD INVENTORY
SCORE SUMMARY

Obsessions Total: _____

Compulsions Total:_____

Intensity Total: _____

Depression Total: _____

KCOCDI INVENTORY SUMMARY SCORE: _____

PART VI: SPECIAL CHACTERISTICS

To truly understand what it means to have an Obsessive Compulsive Disorder in any of its many manifestations (Hypochondriasis, Body Dysmorphic Disorder, and Compulsive Hoarding, etc.) one must look beyond the obsessions, rituals and compulsions that attempt to seduce and imprison the sufferer. While obsessions and compulsions are the hallmark of OCD, "Special Characteristics" affecting self-image, relationships, career, life satisfaction, spirituality, emotional expression, parenting, use of leisure time and many other life areas are often present for the individual with OCD and need to be addressed as part of the recovery process. When one understands obsessive compulsive disorders as neurologically determined errors in the functioning of the basal ganglia region of the brain it is easy to see that having altered brain function can manifest in many ways other than obsessions and compulsions. The assessment of Special Characteristics is based on in-depth interviews with hundreds of people with OCD, reports from many treatment professionals across the U.S., controlled research studies, brain imaging and neuropsychological data. The Special Characteristics have can be divided into three different categories: Lifestyle and Behavior (35 characteristics), Neuropsychological (25 characteristics), and Medical (8 characteristics).

VI-01-SC Loss of spontaneity
None 10—20—30—40—50—60—70—80—90—100 A Lot

VI-02-SC Loss of interest and flattening of mood
None 10—20—30—40—50—60—70—80—90—100 A Lot

VI-03-SC Feelings of being unreal, strange, or disconnected from self
None 10—20—30—40—50—60—70—80—90—100 A Lot

VI-04-SC Loss of natural emotions ("Are these my real feelings or the result of an obsession?"
            "I need to have the same feeling all the time.")
None 10—20—30—40—50—60—70—80—90—100 A Lot

VI-05-SC Picks up new obsessions from others
None 10—20—30—40—50—60—70—80—90—100 A Lot

VI-06-SC Avoids situations which trigger OCD
None 10—20—30—40—50—60—70—80—90—100 A Lot

VI-07-SC Difficulty with sensory-integration (Bothered by sounds, textures, etc.)
None 10—20—30—40—50—60—70—80—90—100 A Lot

VI-08-SC Sense of "It's not Okay to be here", "I've done something wrong", "Being on edge"
None 10—20—30—40—50—60—70—80—90—100 A Lot

VI-09-SC Reassurance seeking ("Tell me it's OK." "Do it this way", "I need the
            information", "We"-type thinking.)
None 10—20—30—40—50—60—70—80—90—100 A Lot

VI-10-SC   Subtle symmetry needs (Lining up media collections. Dressing in all solid colors. Keeping money in order.)
None 10—20—30—40—50—60—70—80—90—100 A Lot

VI-11-SC   Educational or career difficulties
None 10—20—30—40—50—60—70—80—90—100 A Lot

VI-12-SC   Hypervigilance or trust issues
None 10—20—30—40—50—60—70—80—90—100 A Lot

VI-13-SC   Difficulty living in the present
None 10—20—30—40—50—60—70—80—90—100 A Lot

VI-14-SC   Over-focused on the present moment
None 10—20—30—40—50—60—70—80—90—100 A Lot

VI-15-SC   Vacation and travel difficulties / limitations
None 10—20—30—40—50—60—70—80—90—100 A Lot

VI-16-SC   Self-esteem issues, shame, "I'm bad"
None 10—20—30—40—50—60—70—80—90—100 A Lot

VI-17-SC   Fear of the absence of obsessions or compulsions
None 10—20—30—40—50—60—70—80—90—100 A Lot

VI-18-SC   Fear of making decisions
None 10—20—30—40—50—60—70—80—90—100 A Lot

VI-19-SC   Questioning everything
None 10—20—30—40—50—60—70—80—90—100 A Lot

VI-20-SC   Inflexibility. Difficulty with change. All or none thinking. Must have exercise a certain way. Must eat certain foods in a certain order, or "completely"
None 10—20—30—40—50—60—70—80—90—100 A Lot

VI-21-SC   Things seem connected that should not be ("Cognitive Fusion")
None 10—20—30—40—50—60—70—80—90—100 A Lot

VI-23-SC   "Strange" ideas (e.g. "feelings" that stuffed animals are "alive")
None 10—20—30—40—50—60—70—80—90—100 A Lot

VI-24-SC   Problems with remembering if something was done already (can't see in mind)
None 10—20—30—40—50—60—70—80—90—100 A Lot

VI-25-SC   Can't remember how something is supposed to done
None 10—20—30—40—50—60—70—80—90—100 A Lot

VI-26-SC Problems understanding overall idea behind what was discussed earlier
None 10—20—30—40—50—60—70—80—90—100 A Lot

VI-27-SC Problems with visual attention
None 10—20—30—40—50—60—70—80—90—100 A Lot

VI-28-SC Thermal regulation problems
None 10—20—30—40—50—60—70—80—90—100 A Lot

VI-29-SC Trouble identifying smells (microsmia)
None 10—20—30—40—50—60—70—80—90—100 A Lot

VI-30-SC "Feeling-of-doing" judgments (lack of self-awareness of own performance)
None 10—20—30—40—50—60—70—80—90—100 A Lot

VI-31-SC Difficulty or excessive organizing
None 10—20—30—40—50—60—70—80—90—100 A Lot

VI-32-SC Trouble with sequential ordering
None 10—20—30—40—50—60—70—80—90—100 A Lot

VI-33-SC Trouble shifting from one idea to the next
None 10—20—30—40—50—60—70—80—90—100 A Lot

VI-34-SC Impulsive or sudden emotions or acts
None 10—20—30—40—50—60—70—80—90—100 A Lot

VI-35-SC Symptoms worse in AM
None 10—20—30—40—50—60—70—80—90—100 A Lot

VI-36-SC Staying up later at night
None 10—20—30—40—50—60—70—80—90—100 A Lot

VI-37-SC Issues with low self-esteem
None 10—20—30—40—50—60—70—80—90—100 A Lot

VI-38-SC Negative thought patterns which increased anxiety and, or depression
None 10—20—30—40—50—60—70—80—90—100 A Lot

VI-39-SC Difficulty making choices due to doubt
None 10—20—30—40—50—60—70—80—90—100 A Lot

This section is for informational purposes and is not scored.

PART VII: YOUR EXPERIENCE OF ANXIETY

Fear is a natural and balanced response to a real danger in the environment. Anxiety is an unnatural and out-of-proportion response to thoughts about the future or the past. Each of us experience anxiety in different ways. Think of a recent event and how you felt, thought and behaved when you are feeling you're most anxious. Use that information to fill in the blanks below.

MENTAL / THOUGHTS

_____

_____

_____

PHYSICAL / BODY SENSATIONS

_____

_____

_____

EMOTIONAL / FEELINGS

_____

_____

_____

BEHAVIOR CHANGES

_____

_____

_____

PART VIII: CO-EXISTING OBESSIVE-COMPULSIVE SPECTRUM DISORDERS

It is the rule rather than the exception for someone with OCD to have one or more co-existing obsessive compulsive spectrum disorders. Only 8% of persons with OCD have OCD alone. The most frequent co-existing (or comorbid) problems are:

OCD +
Anxiety Disorders (general)	53.0%
Personality Disorders	63.0%
Major Depressive Disorder	28-60.0%
Tourette's Disorder and Tics	6-47.0%
Body Dysmorphic Disorder	33.0%?
Substance Use Disorders (Combined)	29.0%
Hoarding	25-40.0%
Dysthymia	24.4%
Social Phobia	23.0%
Alcohol Abuse (lower than 12% in pop!)	8.0%

There are a variety of assessment instrument available to the clinician to look for the presence of a co-existing OC-Spectrum disorder. It is not our purpose here to assess each in-depth, merely to give a very brief (two question) screening tool. If either item comes up positive, further investigation is warranted. The OCD Recovery Center website provides links to other test materials
(www.ocdrecoverycenter.com)

VII-1-CE Anorexia Disorder (Can be restricting or binging and purging type)

True False I have been unable to maintain body weight at a minimally normal weight for my age and height.

True False I have an intense fear of gaining weight or becoming fat.

VII- 1-CE Asperger's Disorder

Yes No Restricted repetitive and stereotyped patterns of behavior, interests and activities – Differs from OCD where "interest" is ego-dystonic.

Yes No Restricted patterns of interest that is abnormal either in intensity or focus. Persistent preoccupation with parts or objects

Yes No Apparently inflexible adherence to specific, nonfunctional routines or ritual.

VII-3-CE Autistic Disorder

Yes No Qualitative impairment in social interaction, as manifested by at least two of the following:

Yes No Lack of spontaneous seeking to share enjoyment, interests, or achievements.

Yes No Stereotyped and repetitive motor mannerisms (e.g. hand or finger flapping or twisting, or complex whole-body movement.

VII- 4-CE Body Dysmorphic Disorder

Yes No Preoccupation with an imagined defect in appearance. If a slight physical anomaly is present, the person's concern is markedly excessive.

Yes No Often concerned for social consequences, but sometimes only for own self-appraisal (Deserted Island Test).

VII-5-CE Compulsive Buying

True False I feel compelled to buy things even if I do not need them.

True False Sometimes if I do buy something for a while I feel very anxious until I do.

VII-6-CE Hypochondriasis

Yes No Preoccupation with fears of having, or the idea that one has, a serious disease based on the person's misinterpretation of bodily symptoms

Yes No The preoccupation persists despite appropriate medical evaluation and reassurance.

VII-7-CE Obsessive Compulsive Personality Disorder

Yes No Pervasive pattern of preoccupation with orderliness, perfectionism, rules, lists, productivity, miserliness, and mental and interpersonal control beginning by early adulthood.

Yes No Compulsive behavior designed to achieve goal rather than relieve anxiety.

Yes No Compulsive behavior is often useful and productive.

VII-8-CE Trichotillomania (and Compulsive Picking and Pulling Behaviors)

Yes No Recurrent pulling out of one's hair or picking of skin noticeable hair loss or skin damage.

Yes No Strong feelings of shame and low self-esteem related to picking or pulling activity.

Yes No "Signature pattern" for the picking or pulling including prodromal sensations.

VII-9-CE Tourette's Disorder

Yes No Makes sudden, rapid, recurrent non-rhythmic, stereotyped motor movement or vocalization.

Yes No Tics preceded by a sensory premonitory phenomenon without associated cognition.

Yes No Tics occur daily, in bouts, and vary with stress. Spontaneous fluctuations. Tics tend to wax and wane.

Yes No Able to suppress their tics voluntarily for a short time.

Yes No Factors, such as stress, emotion, concentration and relaxation, influence tic frequency and severity.